Ruins & Kingdoms

Ruins & Kingdoms

Jen Rose Yokel

ISBN: 978-1-329-44739-4

Printed in the United States of America.

Acknowledgements

Every Day Poems (www.tweetspeakpoetry.com): “Saudade”

The Molehill: Volume 3 (ed. A.S. Peterson; Rabbit Room Press, 2014) : “When I See It,” “Processional,” “The First Element,” and “It Always Rains in Winter Garden”

The Rabbit Room (www.rabbitroom.com) : “How It All Ends” and “October”

Contents

When I See It

I know poetry when I see it.
It dances and sings and leaps
across the page.
It shapes the white space
breathing life into ink marks and wood pulp.

I know poetry when I see it—
The essence of truth compressed
into a line so small, yet so full.
You read it over and over again
To know it by heart.
You write it down word for word,
letter for letter,
period for period,
for the wonder of what it felt like
to write it.

I know poetry when I see it—
standing on my toes
straining for a glimpse
over the shoulders of giants,
feeling small and speechless
in their presence.

And sometimes—

I feel the surge of words
begging to be set loose.
I hear them whispering
between the notes of a song,
or in the voice of a friend,
or in a flare of epiphany.

I doubt their worth and wonder if they matter,
and if they could mean anything
to anyone
but me.

But I write them
(or at least I try to)
to honor in the smallest way
the poetry I've seen.

Like a little girl
in her mother's heels
five sizes too large.

The Things You Fear the Most

"Start with your childhood, I tell them. Plug your nose and jump in, and write down all your memories as truthfully as you can. Flannery O' Connor said that anyone who has survived childhood has enough material to write for the rest of his or her life." — Anne Lamott

If you want to write you must
first go back to childhood.
Find that time you fell,
or woke to dreams of monsters,
or emerged from the magical world
between shirt racks
to find your mother had vanished.
In those pale pre-dawn memories are the fears,
the shadows that chased you
into your grown-up life.

In there are the seeds
you bring back to plant
into towering,
sheltering forests.
The things you fear the most
are the only things you have.

By Any Other Name

My grandfather's name was a flower,
a thorny token of love.
It was passed to my father
to my mother
to my sister
and me.

I've come to find it
appropriate
to our condition —
romantic, beautiful,
but so very human.

Petals and thorns,
fragile and sharp,
strong as love itself.

Out Front, She Grew Flowers

When Grandma Rose lived in Bassville Park,
we never lacked a babysitter
or a place for family get-togethers.
People gravitated
to her mint green
mobile home,
so tiny,
so fragile
and Floridian,
but to a kid it was
the biggest place in the world.

Mostly, I remember her yard
as huge.
It didn't have
moss-laden oak trees
or places to climb and swing,
but it was spacious
and green
and well kept.

Out front, she grew flowers.
Our favorite was the powderpuff,
bushy with red, fluffy flowers
that floated on breezes
and proclaimed the promise
of nectar to butterflies and bees.
The air-light petals brushed
small hands and cheeks,
but we knew better than
to pluck them
from their home.

Sometimes,
I think about driving
back to her old house.

I told my mom about that one time,
wondering out loud if I could even
remember the street
she lived on.

She said I would,
that sometimes
she's tempted,
but she doesn't
because she's afraid
it changed too much.

Perhaps it did.
But someday, I will,
just to see.

The Ashes of Citizen's Blvd

They're tearing the old bank down —
the glass and concrete walkway,
the sun-faded mosaic murals.
Daily, they're hosing down
the graying dust of progress.

Since I was a child, it stood,
two buildings joined by a
clear skyward road
where suited men, and women in heels
crossed the air about their business.

It would be easier perhaps
if the place burned down,
because an accident destroying
your childhood's landmarks would
somehow be easier to swallow.

Our towns are built to change.
The roads, the buildings
aren't the same anymore.
The houses crumble, overgrown,
and the vacant ones are locked.

I can see the foam-white water
beating those ashes down
as a crane removes
another wall

with almost the same reverence
as a hand closing a casket.

Processional

We make a clumsy march, these machines
gleaming in the winter sun —
a line of old sedans,
hulking SUVs,
and dirt-crusted trucks.

And the leader of our patched-up parade,
is long, stern, and black,
led and followed
by flashing lights.

"There was a time when people pulled over,"
          Dad says,
and on the two lane backroads
they do.

Work trucks, like beasts of burden,
and old beaters with fading paint jobs
slide over and stop
where the dust blows up
scatters
settles
marking us all.

The Story Begins

In the beginning there was a song.
Maybe it was a spoken phrase suspended
over the surface of the waters,
but somehow I'd like to believe instead
that time, space, eternity converged
in one crack in time
in an arpeggio of exploding light
in crescendo.
Let there be.
And it was good.

Absence
(after Gelineau)

We perceive perhaps
    a single percent
    of all that exists
    (say the physicists).
The rest is
    a hungering absence
    terror and great darkness
    un-sensable 99%.

Could it be you're in the darkness too?

Not just in
    the flame of sunsetting
    or my hot blood's pulsing
    or storm clouds unrolling
    as the sky splits, weeps.
Your presence in the absence
    what they call "dark matter,"
        only dark
when you hold back your light
    so the stars prick through.

Psalm

Sometimes music is grace.
Sometimes words alone can only say
I'm not sure I hear you
I'm not sure I know you
I'm not sure I'm not surely
imagining.
Is this why darkest lonely nights
and a king's harp
could reach God's own heart?
Is this why you saw fit
to keep his words alive,
even the bitter ones? Especially those.
Sometimes music is grace.
A vapor-light promise spoken
in a language celestial
that bends down to meet us
while we in
so many frail
words reach
up.

LEAH

I am the consolation prize
the second first
like you.

Will you love me less,
your second choice,
swindled into your arms
till death?

The Road

Don't mind the dust that
dulls your clothes.
It is the color of grace.
Red clay and gray cloud
settles in the fibers
and smears your face.
But all will be made clean.
The servant comes
and washes your feet
with purest water
and heaven's tears.

How It All Ends

She used to say she loved
those TV movies about Jesus,
but hated the crucifixion scene

even though it was toned down
in the grains of 1970s film,
palatable to the eyes of those
eating dinner in front of
a flickering screen.

This is us, now, knowing
how it all ends, knowing
in three days the lungs of God
would reinflate.

Knowing the ending, could I
ever comprehend the blackness,
ever imagine the darkest
Saturday in history?

A King's body shrouded in spices
and linen lay withering
behind stone,

The budding bloom of salvation,
crushed
careless
trod by
His creation.

Oh my God

today the sun scatters clouds
the sun that once turned away
at your final earthly breath,
as the lion lay shorn and still.

May I never forget
the darkest day of history,
spring stopped, waiting,
pressing her face
at the tomb's door.

The First Element

In the beginning
there was nothing
yet your spirit moved
over the waters.

In the end of an age
a flood purged the world.

In the beginning of another
you in the human mold
of earth and air came up
from the river, cleansed.

And your servant trembled
knowing all his baptisms
could never cleanse one
already pure.

In the now
I dare to wade into the ocean
that gives and takes
that plays with children
that wrecks men on the rocks.

A fluid force
a tender tempest
much like you.

The Truth About Falling

is it's not so much a free fall
from a great height,
the wind pulling your hair and skin
in weightless adrenaline.
Maybe we don't fall in love
so much as we float into it.

All I know is, like
the slow unfolding of
a rare flower, petals
warming in the noonday sun,
or waking slowly from
a colorless dream,
catching sight of dust
dancing on a beam of light
on a morning without a clock
to tell you what time it is
or where you need to be,

sometimes, it slips in
through a barely cracked window,
and you don't even notice
until you feel the presence
flood the room with light.

Boston Logan

In the stock exchange of human motion
where they come and go
          come and go

with clacking suitcase wheels,
hello and goodbye,
and business calls
in the chaos of commute,

we have found our still place
in the tyranny of noise
where you breathe against me
and I lean into you

and the turning world around us
couldn't move this moment.

MYSTERY

Let me tell you a mystery.

It began with dust,
        an exhale, awakening.
Then came a rib,
        close to the heart,
        exposed, sewn up.

And the one became two,
stitched soul to soul
by a secret holy thread.

***

I once wondered why
loneliness aches in our chests
as we reach for fragments of glory
and stumble toward hints and guesses.

Then you found me.

You followed the thread
like a forest trail
nearly covered by leaves

or more like a brook,
a single shining strand
lit by the moonlight.

You followed it into
my secret lonely.
You followed me into
my echoing dark.

***

Let me tell you a mystery

how the two become one,
stitched soul to soul
by a secret holy thread.

Ruins & Kingdoms

The hill holds summer's color
as long as it can,
before the rust runoff of
fading leaves, flaking rust
from the tops of trees
stains all the world in a ruin of color,
in beautiful corrosion.

And I will hold you
as long as I can,
in these silent ruins of
season's turning, nature's burning
another year to its end.
The silence is a kind of poetry
and so is the laughter,
filling the hollow of the heart.

Rust and lace and wild roses
are all we have to build our kingdom,
and when the summer hill is
dusted with snow,
and the forest pillars are
painted in white,
and ice bracelets glitter the
bare arms of trees

I will hold you as long as I can.

The key to this kingdom was
unhidden all along
somewhere in the wild roses.

Remember

thou art dust.
Remember
love is alchemy.

The only thing that
can animate ashes.

Incarnation

Now
you embody
every poem I chased
every love song made flesh

I could translate you
for a lifetime
and still
never be fluent.

Trinity

Sometimes we talk about
the tattoos we'd get
if we were brave enough
to take the pain.

For me, a feather,
a wispy thing
strong enough to lift
bodies of birds to the sky,
maybe burning with a
phoenix fire
like hope, life, death, resurrection.

For you, the triquetra,
endlessly looping in itself
like Father, Son, and Spirit
like infinity, mystery, and hope
endless
like my phoenix.

I study the lines of the ring you gave me,
two trinity knots forged by love,
like you and me
and the Pillar of Fire,
love strong
as hope, life, death, resurrection

strong as a white gold tattoo.

UNEXPECTED

It's like that moment
in conversation
when you've got the pleasantries out of the way --

the *Where are you froms* and
What do you dos and
What is up
with this weathers.

Then someone lets it slip they
stay up late scratching out poems,
or sometimes wish they had superpowers,
or always believed that Sam
was the real hero who destroyed the ring
in the end.

Then you couldn't stop the words
with a twelve story dam.
Then you'd carry that person to
the edge of Mordor yourself.

Instant Information

I forgot how to wait
so in bursts I watch the world.
Tiny thought scraps
shot through fiberoptic threads,
a transmission
to those who care to look.
Friends, acquaintances
and a stranger or two (hundred)
tick through a timeline.
I refresh, compulsive,
in tune, first to know
of road trips and broken arms and earthquakes.
It's a matter of convenience.

But is it too much to ask
for a cup of coffee
and a little more than 140 characters?

Commuter Hymn

Sometimes morning comes too early.
The first half is always hardest
between construction-ripped highways
and traffic draining the precious
almost-4-dollar-a-gallon gas.

Most days, I'd like to teleport.
After all, it's not like I'd miss
the beauty. Not much. But what
if I only had eyes to see
the magic in this daily run?

Would I see brake lights as flaming
dragon eyes? A foe to defeat
with freedom's song? Would piles
of rebuilding dirt be mountains,
an adventure to be climbed?

This is the song of the living.
From home to work, and there
and back again. And under it
all, a holy heartbeat trembles
as dust clouds of glory settle.

Weightlessly

Maybe it was
Sigur Rós in the
car speakers
or just a Monday
frame of mind,
seeking sanity
in noise,

but I caught sight of
a plastic Publix bag
drifting on a breeze,
just long enough to see it

billowing, suspended
like a shot
in some slow-moving
indie film,
like a jellyfish
propelling weightlessly.

A faint wind
whispers spring,
and even trash
comes alive.

Fracture

"There's a crack in your mug,"
she said,
noticing one single, sinuous
hairline fracture
etched from top to bottom,

a drip of coffee running through
the subtle curve,
like a two lane
country road
darkened by rain.

But not even a drop
leaked through.
As I washed the mug and
scrubbed the stain
the crack disappeared.

I trace its line, and wonder if
it was ever there,
or how many other
ordinary things
have a web of outside cracks,

a map of fragile places
one tap
away from shattering,
and if nightly I am washing
my own stains away.

HOUSESITTING

Orange peel, blue bowl,
black mug (Darth Vader),
open balcony, clean breeze,
riding on the morning.
Two dogs. None mine.

I make my home anywhere.
Anywhere there are
poems and sunlight
to catch them by.

It Always Rains in Winter Garden

And a storm is never convenient
so we run for the shelter of umbrellas
and storefronts, or wait in warm cars,
wipers clearing the intrusion away.

Summer storms come, fast and feral,
a whorl of wind, lightning, racing clouds
and just as fast, they scatter.

But sometimes it's not all darkness
the clouds like damp wool blankets
wrung out, dripping over city streets.

Sometimes rain spills out with sunshine
pouring down, mingling in liquid light.
It washes the dust from roof and road
and placates the thirsty earth

to raise gardens from our stone and progress,
cleanse cities till they shine like new,
and green a ravaged earth aching for
renewal in the warm and wet.

The drops sparkle as they fill the air
but still we wait it out,
while everything growing beneath our feet
raises its hands and shivers hallelujah.

Until The Chill Comes

Here
there is no unfolding drama,
no banners of autumn
in red, orange, yellow,
to turn the trees sunlike
for just a moment.

Here summer
locks her fingers in green,
clings to lost youth
'til winter has its way.

But the burning beauty in all things
is a slow burn
until it flames out,
until the chill comes

to remind us all things
are destined to bloom again.

October

The light looks different this time of year.
Shafts of gold pierce trees
transient, darkening.
The earth goes to bed
a little earlier each night

because she knows she's getting older,
fighting gravity, remembering
carefree green and dancing in the
rain, remembering emotional
thunder and flashing lightning.

But now,
she's only wiser
and knows sleep makes all things
rested, beautiful.

And tomorrow she'll wake early,
dress in fire red and bands of gold
because she can
with no one left to impress
and never more alive.

First Last Snowfall

This March day is buried in
winter's last ragged breath
and whitewashed bare trees,

and I know you've probably seen enough
after a long winter's
sloshing and shoveling.

But to me
it looks like magic.

Beauty Brigade

Like a color bomb,
an anti-winter weapon,
the wildflowers
explode
on the roadside.

Oh winter,
where is your sting?
A fragile army
overthrows
death's regime.

Young Again

Lazy Saturday mornings,
my cat pushing
curtains open
that couldn't block
the Eastern summer sun
if they tried.

Arms of the green
camphor tree
outside my window
spread like arms
catching a baseball
or accepting sprinkler rain.

Summer once meant more
than longer hotter days.
It was school's ending,
youth and possibility.

And this old earth knows.
As sun and moon
dance around her,
she dresses verdant,
dreams,
grows young again.

Gather

In stillness, thoughts gather,
running rivulets and raindrops.
I have rushed too long
worried too much,
slept too little.

Tonight
I gather them in words
and one by one
release them into the
atmosphere.

Hum

She learned to love the silence
in the spaces
between words
and in the darkness charged
with electric white noise
burning down the wires
on a stormy summer night.
She learned to read the silence
then hum it
into song.
In the holy, lonely
space of it
till every atom
quivers with melody.

Song in the Stillness

An orchestra tunes outside,
but this symphony
is only heard in stillness.

One move, one breath
is enough to drown it out,
though the air is thick,
heavy, and humid
with it.

Where do you go
come the day?
What stills your hymn, and
what moonbright magic
wakes you again?

Or are you always there,
but I am too in motion
to hear what sings all along?

Shadows

Every shadow in the corner
forgotten by the daylight
where flecks of dust gather
and hide in secret
and every lengthening line
that draws trees on the street
on the opposite side of a horizon
going up in flames
holds in the weight of darkness
proof of light and presence.

Tell Me

"Tell me your dream
and I'll tell you mine,"
you said.

I would
but I can't find words.

Don't you know
dreams are flighty things,
abstractions of
yellow, red, green?

They are made of
substance and light
or something like
ink and moonshadows.

QUEEN

I came to write a verse
about the full moon,
and there it is, waiting
at my window,
like a queen waiting
for a court artist
to paint her portrait.
The monarch of the night
climbing, rising,
casting soft, cold light
to my inside world.

It couldn't be more perfect,
but where are the words for
this kind of glory?

It seems far better
to drop the pen,
turn off the light,
listen to the quiet,
be in the moment.

The Other Language

It's been a while
since I listened to silence,
as if there were such a thing,

because there is always motion
vibrations of atom against atom
tiny galaxies jostling each other
in the brushed silvery surface of my lamp
or the chipped faux wood nightstand.

Like tonight, I can hear the faint echo of crickets
somewhere outside my window
harmonizing with the occasional whoosh
of passing cars, and a little bit closer to me,
my cat taps out a sort of lap and swallow rhythm
while she drinks water from her bowl.

Not to mention the whirr of a laptop fan
and the scratch of pen against paper
forming ink into words as I try
to find silence's most faithful translation.

Tiffany Chapel: 1893

I.

This sacred space
feels so much bigger
inside,

and your "temple of art"
could be a place
of worship.

Because in every shard of mosaic,
in every electrified crystal,
in every bend of colored light,

I swear I could see straight to heaven
through the painted eyes of the Virgin,
through the eyes of peacock feathers.

II.

All things fall into disrepair,
withered grass, and falling night.

Morning comes
light slanting from the east.

The fog burns away
and dew glitters the earth.

I blink at the wonder
of a world turned mosaic.

The Garden

Go, said the bird, for the leaves were full of children,
Hidden excitedly, containing laughter.
Go, go, go, said the bird: human kind
Cannot bear very much reality. ~ T. S. Eliot, "Burnt Norton"

I went down one day to the garden gate
just to hear the voices laughing
because I missed some part of the past,
forgot what it felt to be young, though
I am not so old. The sun warmed the air
and I breathed deep memories of the garden,
listening for a blue jay, wondering where they've gone,
when I last heard the call of that wild bird.
Somewhere in the trees his voice is hidden.
Go, said the bird, for the leaves were full of children,

playing hide and seek with my memories
and I hear the past in the rustling leaves
remembering summer days, when the sprinklers
were glittering curtains for cooling, splashing,
and clouds became walking mountains in the sky,
and maybe we could catch them, running after
something like being grown up.
What do you want to be? They call,
as if the future were something I could capture,
hidden excitedly, containing laughter.

Could I go back? I couldn't, but would I
when time, time, time marches ever on?
Would I steal a draught from a dried-up fountain
of youth, just to run with them again?
Could we untaste Eden's tainted fruit?
Remembering the pure and innocent mind,
but knowing the depths of wonder now,
would I trade it all for a sip, to turn back
the clock? But when I asked for more time,
go, go, go, said the bird: human kind

is the only creature preoccupied
with deadlines and long-term goals,
with settling down and making something
of ourselves. What if we saw time
not as a thing to race or run out,
not cash to manage, or temporary?
All is short but I hear my beginning
singing toward my end. She's there
and I know, somehow this ghostly mortality
cannot bear very much reality.

The Lilac Wood

"The unicorn lived in a lilac wood, and she lived all alone."

Some say only a virgin soul
undulled by the world
and the unbearable weight of naming things
will see cloven prints
in the fallen snow.

An old mare shakes her head.
Is she one of them instead?

"Go down to the edge of the wood,"
        she said.
"Go breathe the ancient, wild peace.
Go hear the whirring beat
        of a thousand humming bees."

But the lilac wood waits silent,
cut down and frozen over.

The flow of an eternal spring
will soon split a crack in winter's back
shattered ice, shattered spell
and the curse turns backwards on itself.

Saudade

Like ghosts become flesh for the first time
we came to the land of the living
tasted the bread
sipped the wine
spoke the language of belonging.

In a tent on a hill walled by green
we gathered for one more meal.
I watched twilight
dance with candlelight
and breathed in a hint of truly alive.

Can you be sick for home you've never seen?
Sometimes the curtain flutters,
and I catch a glimpse
of a fawn in the shadow
that bids me to follow.

I can't. Not yet.
But I am coming home.

www.ingramcontent.com/pod-product-compliance
Ingram Content Group UK Ltd.
Pitfield, Milton Keynes, MK11 3LW, UK
UKHW041838200726
13854UKWH00003BA/1204